Motorcycles

by Dee Ready

Content Consultant:
National Motorcycle Museum
and Hall of Fame
Sturgis, South Dakota

Bridgestone Books

an imprint of Capstone Press

Bridgestone Books are published by Capstone Press
818 North Willow Street, Mankato, Minnesota 56001
http://www.capstone-press.com

Library of Congress Cataloging-in-Publication Data
Ready, Dee.
     Motorcycles/by Dee Ready.
     p. cm.
     Includes bibliographical references and index.
     Summary: Briefly describes several types of motorcycles, including touring bikes,
mopeds, and trail bikes.
     ISBN 1-56065-611-5
     1. Motorcycles--Juvenile literature. [1. Motorcycles.] I. Title.
TL440.15.R43   1998
629.227'5--dc21

                                                    97-12196
                                                       CIP
                                                       AC

Photo credits
Cheryl Blair, 6, 18
Betty Crowell, 10
FPG/Luis Rosendo, 16
Timothy Halldin, cover
International Stock/Peter Langone, 8
Unicorn Stock/Robert Ginn, 12; Jeff Greenberg, 14; Eric Berndt, 20
Yamaha, 4

Table of Contents

Motorcycles

A motorcycle is like a bicycle. They both have the same shape. But a motorcycle is bigger and heavier. It is powered by an engine. An engine is a machine that moves a motorcycle.

Road Motorcycles

A road motorcycle is made to travel on roads. It is used for everyday travel. People use road motorcycles to get to work or school. Road motorcycles have seats for one or two riders.

Cruisers

A cruiser is a road motorcycle with extra parts. Some extra parts might be horns or special seats. People add whatever they want. Cruisers are often bright colors. They have a lot of chrome. Chrome is a shiny metal.

Touring Motorcycles

A touring motorcycle is used to take trips. It is big enough for two riders. A touring motorcycle has space for suitcases. It is the most comfortable motorcycle. Comfortable means easy to sit on.

Police Motorcycles

Some police officers ride motorcycles. Their motorcycles have red and blue lights. They use their motorcycles to patrol roads. They use motorcycles to help keep roads safe.

Motor Scooters

A motor scooter has two or three wheels. It rides low to the ground. Its wheels are smaller than road motorcycle wheels. A motor scooter also has a small engine.

Mopeds

A moped has pedals like a bicycle. A pedal is pushed with the foot. Pedals help the engine. They can also move the moped if the engine stops. Mopeds can go a long way on a little gas.

Dirt Bikes

A dirt bike is made to travel off of roads. It can travel on uneven ground. A dirt bike has special wheels. The wheels have bumps called nubs. The nubs help the bike travel over hills and rocks.

ATVs

ATV stands for All-Terrain Vehicle. Terrain is ground or land. ATVs have four wheels. They can travel on all kinds of ground. ATVs can carry people to places that are hard to reach.

Hands On: How a Motorcycle Balances

People can balance moving motorcycles on two wheels. Balance means to stand up and not fall over. But motorcycles do not balance when they are not moving. Try this test to find out why.

What You Need:
One quarter
A flat place like a table

What You Do:
1. Try to make the quarter stand on its edge. It will not stand up.
2. Now hold the quarter on its edge with your finger.
3. Use another finger to spin the quarter. The quarter will balance while it spins.

The quarter will balance as long as it is spinning. This is just like a motorcycle. The motorcycle will balance as long as its wheels are spinning.

Words to Know

chrome (KROHM)—a shiny metal

comfortable (KUHM-fur-tuh-buhl)—easy to sit on

engine (EN-juhn)—a machine that moves things like motorcycles

nub (NUHB)—a bump on a wheel that helps it hold to the ground

terrain (tuh-RAYN)—ground or land

Read More

Barrett, N. S. *Motorcycles*. New York: Franklin Watts, 1984.

Cooper, Jason. *Motorcycles*. Vero Beach, Fla.: Rourke, 1991.

Flint, Russ. *All About Motorcycles*. Milwaukee: Gareth Stevens, 1990.

Internet Sites

The Bike Page

http://www2.euronet.nl/users/pa3fvw/bike.html

The Master Link Page

http://www.ultramall.com/Bikes/thelist.html

Index